In the Weeds

A Guide to Saving Your Own Soul on This Crazy Journey Called Motherhood

CINDY CAPRIO WOULFE

ISBN: 978-1-964377-95-7 (ebook)

ISBN: 978-1-964377-96-4 (paperback)

ISBN: 978-1-964377-97-1 (hardcover)

Scan the QR code below to access your free *In the Weeds* Mom's Emergency Self-Care Plan

Contents

For Winston & Hudson, the beautiful souls I am lucky enough to call my sons. Thank you for being my greatest teachers. I love you more than anything in the whole world.

xo

INTRODUCTION

One Tuesday night early in my motherhood journey, I had just finished up with the "momming" part of the day—I had tucked in my then two-year-old son and he was sleeping soundly. I had picked up all his toys and put them away, washed the dinner dishes and cleaned the kitchen. My husband wasn't home from work yet, and I finally had time to myself after a long day of wishing for time to myself. I felt so lost, so completely out of energy, that sitting there in the dark was all I could manage. I found myself sitting in my son's child-sized Pottery Barn chair in my clean, quiet kitchen, looking around and thinking, *What is wrong with me?*

Looking back, I realize that moment in that tiny chair wasn't just exhaustion—I was *in the weeds*.

Years earlier, I had worked at a very busy upscale sports bar and restaurant in New York City, directly across from the Empire State Building and two blocks down from Madison Square Garden. The location made it a prime spot to grab a drink pre- or post-game, concert or convention—or to sit down for a full meal. These busy nights were my first real experience of being in the weeds.

In the restaurant world, being in the weeds means that you're so slammed with orders that you are completely overwhelmed and overstimulated. It's a crazy feeling, and no matter how many times I found myself in the moment when I thought I might drown, I didn't—and each time I didn't, I was greatly rewarded with a wad of cash, tired feet and a sense of accomplishment. Nobody ever told me that motherhood could feel so much like that old familiar sensation of being in the weeds—except with a house, a baby and nobody else to cover my tables—and minus the wad of cash. Perhaps you can relate?

Maybe you just had a baby and you're trying to find your groove. Maybe you sailed through your first little one but now that you have two, you feel like you're drowning. Maybe your kids are big now, but a part of you is wondering where *you* went—the you before motherhood. Maybe you're hoping to get pregnant, or you're newly expecting and want to feel as prepared as possible. Or maybe you're sitting in your own dark kitchen, trying to figure out why you feel so overwhelmed. Whatever the case, you are not alone, and there is hope for you here.

This is a good time to tell you that this is *not* a parenting book. There are plenty of those out there already, and if you're feeling overwhelmed with parenting, chances are you've already read one—or 10—of them. I'm not here to tell you how to get your baby to sleep through the night, whether to breastfeed or bottle-feed or how much screen time is too much. This book is for *you*. How are *you*? When was the last time someone asked you that? My guess is...when you were pregnant. In fact, pregnancy might be the time in your life when you're asked that the most—even by strangers. But when you become a mom, the question shifts to, "How's the baby?" or "How are the kids doing?" And for good reason—those little ones are adorable and need a lot of love and care. But I'm here to talk about *you*. Because, in case you haven't heard it in a while—*you* matter, too. You—the one who likely grew the baby, and are now feeding the baby, pouring your time, energy, sleep and body into this little human. And in case no one has told you in a while: *you are doing a beautiful job.* Of course, you love your children. But two things can be true at once. You can love your children *and* feel like this is *so* hard. Your heart and hands can be full, and your soul can still feel completely drained. And that's okay.

In the pages that follow, I've shared both big and small ways that have helped me stay sane and centered on those overwhelming days—the ones where it all feels like *too much.*

There's no right way to read this book. If you want to take it all in at once, go for it! But if you're like me, you'll probably read it in little bits—with your morning coffee, while your baby is sleeping in your arms or for a few quiet minutes before bed. While you can move through it however feels right, I encourage you to think of it as a daily practice. Use it as a little ritual for yourself. If you take the time to reflect and complete a journal prompt each day, in 30 days, I hope you'll feel more balanced—and maybe even discover a new side of yourself that you can apply to other areas of your life. That said, you can use this book however it feels best for *you*. Because that is the main message I want you to get from this book—you matter, too!

Maybe it becomes a quiet place to write and reflect—a journal experience where you can start to hear your own voice again. Or maybe you dive right in, plowing through all of the chapters first and then returning when you're ready to complete each journal prompt, one at a time. If journaling feels like too much for you right now, maybe just read it and let the stories and lessons sit with you for a while. There's no pressure, no wrong way to show up. Wherever you are in your motherhood journey, I hope this book meets you there. Let this be something you look forward to and take at your own pace, not just another thing on your to-do list. Think of this as one of the first steps to putting yourself first. It is my hope that this can also be a gentle reminder that you are not alone in this beautiful chaos. Let's get you thriving, not just surviving on this crazy journey called motherhood.

My hope is that this book makes things just a little easier. Not the parenting part—I'm raising two boys of my own, and I can tell you, that part will probably always feel a little hard. But let this book help with the "taking care of *you*" part. Because one thing I know for sure—the more you care for yourself and fill your own soul, the better you can show up, take care of your children and nurture their little souls, too.

DAY 1:
IT'S OKAY TO NOT BE OKAY

It was our first month in a new house, in a new state, with a new baby and a toddler. Outside, it was the third straight day of very cold, very icy weather so we weren't going anywhere. My three-year-old wasn't in preschool yet since we were so new in town, and my nine-month-old was crawling up a storm, getting into everything. From before sunup to after sundown, my main mission was to keep both boys fed, alive and safe from the stairs and each other. Each day felt like a real-life version of *Groundhog Day*.

That morning, I got a text from across the country from my good friend, Brook, checking in on how we were settling into the new house—and how I was doing. How *was* I doing? I wondered. I decided to be honest and confess that maybe I had no idea what I was doing and that I felt like I was losing my mind a bit. Obviously, I was not doing motherhood "right."

Her response is something I will never forget:

"Motherhood can be a dark hole sometimes."

With those seven words, I had never felt so seen and validated! If Brook, who seemed to have her life together—two kids older than mine, a life filled with travel and fun—could say that, then maybe I wasn't alone. Maybe there wasn't anything wrong with me—or the kind of mom I was. Maybe this is just motherhood sometimes.

She reassured me that things would get better—that once my oldest started preschool and I could safely leave the house more often, things would look up. And she was right! My son started preschool three mornings a week, my husband finally installed all the baby gates (no more stair-related panic attacks!), the ice melted and the sun returned. I could literally see the light again.

I have never forgotten my friend's words and the freedom, reassurance and confidence they gave me. It's okay to not be okay sometimes. Motherhood can be a dark hole, but you are not alone in it. It doesn't mean you're doing it wrong. The light will return, and when it does, you'll find your flow again.

See page 132 for journal prompt.

DAY 2:
TAKE A BREAK
BEFORE YOU BREAK

After I pushed my first baby out, I was left with a *"cluster of hemorrhoids."* I know—TMI, totally gross and pretty painful. My doctor's advice for the first month postpartum was a nightly sitz bath.

Every night, I had to fill a little tray with warm water and Epsom salts, set it on the toilet and just sit for 20 minutes, letting everything soak. Then, I'd follow it with a warm shower. At first, the whole thing seemed impossible. Did I really have to just sit alone on the toilet for 20 minutes every night—on top of everything else? I normally spent as little time on the toilet as possible—quick in and out. How was I supposed to manage this extra task while caring for a tiny human and everything that came with it?

But I was in pain and uncomfortable, so I had no choice but to follow the doctor's orders.

After the first few nights of the baby crying and my husband stressing that the baby only wanted me, we finally found our flow and those 20 minutes became everything. My first baby didn't like for me to put him down, even when he was sleeping. He felt safest in my arms, and I was happy to hold him, all day, every day. It was a beautiful season of motherhood, but it also sometimes left me feeling like I was never off duty, never having free arms.

Those 20 minutes of my sitz bath became guaranteed time for myself. I wasn't sleeping, watching TV, cooking, cleaning or holding a baby—I was just *sitting*. Alone. In my bathroom. And it was *non-negotiable* because it was medically necessary—a forced time-out. It was quiet and peaceful. Before long, I started to actually look forward to my nightly sitz bath and shower. What had started as an embarrassing predicament and an extra chore became a quiet and peaceful time that I came to enjoy each night. This was my first real experience of self-care and personal time in motherhood.

Had it not been for my cluster of hemorrhoids and my doctor's orders, I may never have given myself that time.

So, please consider this book your doctor's orders—if you're lucky enough not to have your own hemorrhoids. Mental health is just as important as physical health, and it should be prioritized. Your prescription? Twenty minutes of uninterrupted time alone every day. Mindful, quiet time, no sleeping, no reading, no cleaning, no TV—just quiet. If that sounds impossible, that means you need it even more.

Your nervous system *needs* silence to recharge. Your mind and body *need* a reset–especially when you care for another human 24/7. We'll get to more radical self-care later, but this daily 20-minute pause for mindful quiet time is an excellent place to start.

You deserve it. And trust me, your body and mind will thank you.

See page 134 for journal prompt.

DAY 3:
FIND YOUR PEOPLE

When my youngest was three months old, we were selling our first house and building our next home in another state. My husband was commuting from New Jersey to Connecticut every day, leaving at 5:30 in the morning and not getting home until 8:30 at night. Like clockwork, the baby would wake up the second the garage door closed as my husband left. Two hours later, my two-year-old would join us and the three of us would spend the day together.

Those days were precious, but they were also some of the longest of my life.

On weekends, when my husband was home and able to spend time with the boys when he had not seen them during waking hours all week, I would take an hour during my oldest son's nap, leave the baby with my husband, grab my journal or a book and just go. I would usually find myself at a café with a cup of coffee, savoring every uninterrupted minute to myself.

I remember telling a family member how much that one good hour and uninterrupted coffee break did for my soul. It was met with, *"What about your husband? When does he get a break?"*

My heart sank. Then, I saw red. *His break? His break from what?!*

Yes, he was commuting long hours and working hard all day to financially support us. But every weekend was his break from all that. Every weekday, he drank his coffee hot, went out to lunch and to the bathroom by himself all day long. Then, he drove home alone in a quiet car. And honestly, in those early years as a mother, even a solo bathroom trip or a car ride all alone felt like a break to me.

By the time my second baby came along, I knew when I needed a recharge. I had rarely taken breaks with my first (once my hemorrhoids healed, anyway), but this time, I recognized that I deserved that hour to myself. My arms and mind were full all day, every day. And every single time I took it, I came home better for it.

And you deserve a break too.

If someone in your life makes you feel guilty for that, then they are *not* your people. They can still be your mom, your sister, your best friend. But if they make you feel judged for needing time for yourself, they are not your people for *this*.

Find someone you can call on the hard days. Someone who's been there—or who is in it right now. Someone who gets it, or at the very least, gets you enough to see that you need a break and will be better for it. Someone who will validate your feelings, not make you question them.

Pay attention to how you feel after you vent to someone. If you hang up the phone feeling *worse*, feeling judged or feeling guilty for needing even a little time to yourself, stop calling them for this. You can still love them, talk to them about other things, but just not *this*.

See page 136 for journal prompt.

DAY 4:
FIND YOUR ZEN WHEREVER YOU CAN

Before becoming a mom, I made time to enjoy the little things—a hot cup of coffee, an evening walk with my favorite music, a glass of wine by the fireplace on a Friday night. But once I became a mom, my days looked completely different. My priorities shifted, and for a while, I felt like I was in survival mode.

Is the baby fed? Check. Changed? Check. Clean? Check.

Rinse and repeat.

But I was missing a checklist for myself.

One Saturday morning, when my husband was home, I handed over my sleeping son after a feeding, made a fresh cup of coffee and took it outside. Just one quiet cup of coffee, alone, with the crisp fall air and changing leaves, no one in sight, felt absolutely amazing. That one moment became my Saturday morning ritual and from there, I added on. I updated my playlist and started taking an afternoon stroller walk every day, my favorite music in my headphones. I started lifting weights again in my living room, making funny faces at my son in his little Boppy chair between reps. And eventually, when he started napping in his crib, I used that time to meditate before tackling chores or other naptime tasks.

Slowly, I felt my sense of zen return. And I also noticed something else—on days when I missed one of these little rituals, I felt different. That's when I knew that these moments weren't luxuries; they were important for my mood, and I did everything I could to keep them going consistently.

Do not underestimate the power of the little things. Small moments of appreciation for yourself and your own well-being add up. They reinforce your worth, your happiness and contentment and your perception of value for yourself and your own time.

See where you can add in a simple ritual, or two or three, that make you feel better and commit to them each day. You are still caring for your baby or children, but now you are also incorporating caring for yourself—and that gives you back a sense of personal power and fulfillment.

In the end, it's the little things that matter most.

See page 138 for journal prompt.

DAY 5: WHEN IN DOUBT, DANCE!

When my boys were one and three, they were constantly on the move. Living in Connecticut, our winters can be long and cold, and some days, the weather just wasn't great for getting out of the house. To keep things lively, I often played music in the background while they were playing. Eventually, the music led to dancing, which also led to just running in circles and burning off some serious energy.

I noticed that the moment I turned on the music, the whole vibe in our house shifted. Our dance breaks became a daily ritual, a fun way for the boys to get their wiggles out. What really surprised me was how much I started to look forward to dancing time, too. The music, the dancing and the laughter lightened the mood in our house so much. It gave us a way to move our bodies, be silly and laugh together. It was about connection, a way for us to share pure, silly joy, especially in those early years before any self-consciousness came into play for my boys.

Even as my boys have gotten older, they always request to have music playing. They'll head out to the swings in the backyard, blasting songs from our outdoor speaker, and I can hear their laughter drifting in through the open door. It's a reminder of just how powerful music and movement can be. It shakes things up, raises your vibration and can completely transform the energy of your home.

And let's be real, there's only so much "Wheels on the Bus" a parent can take. I never limited our playlists to kids' music. I always incorporated the music I like, too, which includes all different genres. You get to be the DJ of your house. Feeling tired? Play something upbeat and dance it out. Feel like chaos is everywhere? Try something soothing and relaxing. Even babies love to dance! Both of my boys giggled endlessly when I twirled them around in my arms, until they grew and found dancing feet of their own.

So, when in doubt—dance!

See page 140 for journal prompt.

DAY 6: THIS TOO SHALL PASS

In those first few weeks after bringing our newborn home, if the TV was on, it was either *Golden Girls* or *Everybody Loves Raymond* reruns—comfort food for the soul. But I remember every time someone on the show would announce they were going to bed or say goodnight, I'd think to myself, *That will never be me again. I will never be able to just say goodnight and go to bed again.*

I know that sounds completely ridiculous now—of course, I go to bed all the time. But at that moment, it felt drastic. The endless cycle of nighttime feedings and a crying baby made sleep feel like a thing of the past. As soon as the sun went down, I'd start dreading another marathon night.

And then, like magic, at around four months, my son slept through the night. I actually woke up confused, then had a moment of panic and went to make sure he was still breathing. And there he was, my little baby, well-rested, cooing and smiling up at me, almost as if he knew just how monumental this moment was: *eight whole hours* of sleep.

Just like that, the heavy sea parted.

That's the best way I can describe most phases of babyhood and motherhood—every phase passes eventually. The things that feel impossibly hard in the moment eventually become easier, sometimes without you even realizing it. The only constant is change. And remembering that is what gets you through those long, dark nights. It's also what helps you appreciate those magical moments, because again, nothing stays the same forever.

This knowledge is power. And this reminder? It's life-changing.

See page 142 for journal prompt.

DAY 7: REST IS BEST

Back to those crazy, sleepless nights of newborn feedings, the ones we know will eventually pass! So much feeling lost or crazy in those first few months comes down to one thing: sleep deprivation. There's a reason it's used as a form of torture—nothing feels right when you haven't slept enough. Your physical, mental and emotional health take a serious hit when you are sleep deprived. Reminding yourself of this can help you extend some grace to yourself when everything feels off, when you snap at your partner or when you just can't seem to stop crying.

When we had our first baby, I did not prioritize sleep. *"Sleep when the baby sleeps"* still makes no sense to me—but if you can pull it off, go for it! The key is to fit in sleep *wherever* you can.

When my firstborn was three weeks old, my husband had to go on a weeklong work trip abroad. I took the baby and our dog and went to stay at my mom's house just so I would have support. Being so new to motherhood, I was scared to be alone. She offered to help in any way she could, and I accepted her help to run out for diapers or cook dinner. I was so grateful for these things, but what I needed most was sleep. I did not ask for it. I trusted my mom to care for my baby, but I was too stubborn to admit that I couldn't do it on my own.

When someone you trust asks what they can do to help, don't be a hero—take the nap! One big difference between my first and second baby was that by the second time around, I had learned this. I was still sleep-deprived and running on fumes, but I knew to ask for help when I felt like my world was crumbling.

If you feel like you're losing your mind or the darkness feels like it's closing in—*especially* if you feel the darkness closing in—sleep! Prioritize sleep over everything else. Before you make any decisions, get one good night's sleep before assessing how you're feeling. One good night does wonders and puts you back in a position to think more clearly. It's like hitting the reset button, helping you feel more balanced. Now is the time to speak up about what you need—don't just pretend you're fine. Speak to your partner or someone you trust and be very honest about your need for one full night of sleep.

And if you *do* get a good night's sleep and the darkness still doesn't feel lighter, please speak openly and honestly to your doctor. Postpartum hormones, sleep deprivation and intrusive thoughts can take a serious toll on your mental and physical health, and there is no shame in seeking medical intervention. Just like you'd advocate for your baby, advocate for yourself.

You matter, too.

See page 144 for journal prompt.

DAY 8:
STOP GIVING A F*CK
WHAT OTHER PEOPLE THINK

I was on a plane recently, flying from NYC to Phoenix, when, just after takeoff, a baby started loudly crying. The mom, holding her baby, was doing everything in her power to soothe her baby, but the seatbelt sign was on, and she had to stay put.

I watched as passengers around her grew visibly irritated, giving her disapproving looks, shaking their heads and holding their ears. The poor mom looked mortified. Not only was she trying to figure out what her baby needed (*Was the baby scared? Tired? Hungry? Was the pressure hurting the baby's ears?*), she also had to deal with half the plane judging her and complaining.

My first instinct was to catch her eye and offer my support—a smile, a reassuring glance, a look of concern for both her and the baby, completely free of judgment. When she caught my eye, I saw her exhale. The baby didn't stop crying, but for a brief moment, she felt supported by another mother and, hopefully, shielded from the waves of judgment coming her way.

You have enough to worry about with your own child. There is no room for others' judgment. It's a given: It will always be there. You can do everything perfectly and you'll still offend some people just by hauling your kid around. Some people don't like children. Some people only had children that "never behaved that way." Some people are struggling with their own fertility, and your baby will be a painful reminder of that. You will never know what is going on with someone else, but that judgment is about them, not you.

I promise you—the more you prioritize your connection with your child above all else, the less you will care what people around you think. It's an added stress you do not need. And you will be a better mom for it. Of course, you want to eventually teach your children to be considerate of other people, but being considerate and worrying what other people think are two different things. The sooner you can train your mind to not give a f*ck what other people think, the more confident you will become with your own decisions for your child and the more gracefully you will be able to handle the inevitable stressful situations or meltdowns in public and remain focused on what your child needs instead of what will make other people happy.

This also has the added benefit of carrying over to other things in your life. The freedom of not giving a f*ck what other people think is so liberating. Once you start, you'll realize it starts to show up in other areas of your life, too. It's like a muscle—and once you work it, it will get stronger and stronger. Just one of the many ways in which becoming a parent helps you become a better version of yourself.

See page 146 for journal prompt.

DAY 9: CHOOSE ONE THING

When my oldest was two and my youngest was four months old, life felt like a whirlwind. My husband had just started a new job and we were in the middle of selling our home and moving to another state—everything felt out of control.

One day, I came across an article about committing to running just one mile a day. The idea was simple: If you can run at all, you can run a mile. That's all—no more, no less.

I had a relatively easy time losing my pregnancy weight, especially after my second, mostly because I was too busy keeping two humans alive to feed myself anyway. But I still felt like I was in a rut both physically and emotionally. I figured running a mile a day would help tighten things up and help me get back to the body that felt strong. The only problem was I had no idea where I was going to fit in a mile run each day while being solely in charge of two little humans.

But I needed something. So I accepted the challenge.

What started as just a fun little experiment eventually completely changed my outlook. Most mornings, I'd put the baby down for his nap, bring my two-year-old outside with the baby monitor and run laps in the driveway or backyard. My toddler loved it and he'd often run alongside me, giggling and cheering me on.

The beauty of this challenge was that it became nonnegotiable for me. I had committed to one mile a day and I didn't want to miss a single day. Some days, life got in the way—someone was sick, the weather was bad or the day just slipped away from me. So, I adapted. I softly jogged laps around the house or I ran laps in the basement after the kids went to bed. I made it work and it became something I actually looked forward to every day.

Physically and mentally, it helped me immensely. A mile a day isn't a monumental feat, but when you add it up, day after day, that's seven miles a week, 30 miles a month. Endorphins are a real thing, and they were pumping through my body every day. Even just one mile a day had such a positive effect on my mood, gave me some purpose each day and helped me burn off stress. More than anything, I think I needed to prove to myself that I could stick to something, that my body was capable of more than just making babies and that I could feel empowered again in my own life.

All it takes is one thing. One change. One challenge you accept and follow through on.

If your physical health is where you need a shift, I invite you to try the one-mile-a-day club. Or come up with your own challenge! But just one thing—no more, no less.

When life feels overwhelming and out of control, it's tempting to make a big list of all the drastic changes that you want to make in your life. But the one-thing rule takes the pressure off. Instead of trying to change everything, just commit to one simple challenge that you can take on and make it nonnegotiable. Your body will thank you.

See page 148 for journal prompt.

DAY 10: DRESS FOR THE PART

I still remember my first hair appointment after having my first child. During pregnancy, I'd avoided the salon and stopped getting highlights because I was extra cautious about all the chemicals. No judgment at all—plenty of women continue with hair maintenance during pregnancy, and their babies turn out just fine. For me, skipping the salon felt like an easy sacrifice, and I still felt good with my luscious pregnancy hair.

The day of my appointment, I took a shower, put on real clothes, and actually blow-dried my hair. Walking out of the house—and later, out of the salon—I felt like a million bucks. I hadn't realized how long it had been since I'd felt that way. I'm not someone who wears a lot of makeup anyway, so motherhood hadn't changed my appearance drastically, but that appointment was the reminder I needed that when I look good, I feel good.

Now, that salon visit didn't turn me into someone who blow-dries my hair and pulls out my tall boots every day. But I did invest in a good dry shampoo and took a long, honest look at my new mom wardrobe. In those early weeks, my pajamas and "real clothes" had basically merged into one comfy blur. And while being comfortable was great, I realized I needed a little more effort to feel like myself again.

Luckily, we live in a time when it's easier than ever to look good *and* be comfortable. Athleisure and stylish loungewear are everywhere. I remember thinking the same thing while I was pregnant too. A look back to decades past when pregnant women stayed home or wore giant tent dresses to hide their bellies shows how much times have changed. I felt lucky to show off my bump and wear cute maternity jeans without feeling like I had to hide anything.

This is the perfect time to figure out your "mom style." For me, it meant putting together a capsule closet (thank you, Marie Kondo!). I chose pieces that felt great, were baby-friendly and helped me feel a little more put together. Every morning, I'd change out of my pjs, pull together an outfit from my capsule wardrobe and brush my hair, adding a little swipe of lip gloss if I was leaving the house. It made such a difference in my mood and my day.

Now, I'm not saying you need to start worrying about how you look in addition to everything else you have going on. But if you haven't been feeling like yourself, this is a simple, doable change that can get you closer to feeling like yourself again. When you look good, you feel good—and how you feel matters too.

Another thing worth mentioning is that comfortable, stylish clothing is a great way to transition back into your pre-baby wardrobe. The last thing a new mom needs is pressure to "bounce back" to her pre-baby size. Every body is different, and comfortable clothing is a great way to look and feel good during that transition. Even though I returned to my usual weight fairly quickly, I kept my maternity jeans in rotation because they were so comfortable and made me feel good.

I want you to feel good too—because when you look good, you feel good!

See page 150 for journal prompt.

Day 11:
YOU CAN'T MAKE
THIS SH*T UP

I once had to call the cops on myself. When my oldest was just three and my baby wasn't quite one, we had found a nice little rhythm to our routine. After breakfast and playtime, I'd put the baby down for a nap upstairs, then come downstairs for two precious hours of one-on-one time with my toddler. Usually, that meant Play-Doh or an art project.

One morning, I got the baby down and told my three-year-old that I was going to go to the bathroom quickly before Play-Doh time. I'd gotten into the habit of leaving the bathroom door open so I could keep an eye on the boys—and also to avoid them banging down the door while I was away from them for 30 seconds.

But that particular day, it had taken a little extra time to get my teething baby down, and my toddler wasn't thrilled about waiting. As I was going to the bathroom, he ran up, slammed the door and pushed up the bottom part of the latch. We had just babyproofed the house and every single door and cabinet had a baby-proof latch on it—including the one I was now locked in. I could hear him giggling on the other side, totally unaware of what he had just done.

Here's the thing about baby-proof locks that you may already know: they're easy for little hands to close but nearly impossible for those same little hands to open. You need to press a side button while simultaneously squeezing two other parts together. A task definitely designed for grown-ups.

So there I was—trapped. Thankfully my baby was asleep upstairs, but my three-year-old was on the other side of the door frantically trying to undo the trick he pulled on me while I tried to calmly relay instructions on how to open the lock that is not made to be opened by little three-year-old hands.

I tried not to panic but my mind was racing, desperately searching for a solution to my predicament. *What am I going to do? Can I break the door down? What if the baby wakes up while I'm stuck in here? I'll have to call for help, where's my phone? OMG my phone is somewhere in the kitchen. Will it fit under the door?*

I instructed my son to look for my phone in the kitchen and try to slide it under the door. It didn't fit. Then I tried to teach him to swipe up and enter the passcode. No luck, he had never used a touch screen before and couldn't get the screen to open. And, of course, we don't have a landline. Now I was starting to panic.

I shoved my shoulder into the door, like I'd seen people do in movies. It didn't budge. I glanced at the bathroom window, my only other option. We were on the first floor, but it was raised and it was still quite a drop right onto the air conditioning unit. Not enough to kill me, but definitely enough to break something—and how could I take care of two little boys with a broken leg?

Then I saw it—our grocery cart cover. I had washed it the day before and it was now hanging on the shower door to dry. I had an idea.

Through the door, I instructed my three-year-old to drag a stool over to the sliding door in the kitchen, unlock it, step out onto the deck and go out to the snow-covered grass just below the bathroom window. He did exactly as he was told.

Luckily, we had been trying on his new boots just that morning and he still had them on.

Once he was in place, I carefully hung myself out the window and slowly lowered the shopping cart cover down with a long scarf that had also been drying tied to it. He then placed my cell phone in the Velcro pocket of the cover and I very slowly pulled it up. One wrong move and my phone would have fallen into the snow! But alas, it worked!

I grabbed the phone and immediately called my husband. No answer. He was an hour away in a meeting. We'd only just moved into the neighborhood and it had been covered with ice and snow, so I hadn't had a chance to get to know anyone well enough to have their cell numbers. I had no choice but to call the police and tell them to come around back because I couldn't get to the front door.

I'll never forget the officer's face as he cautiously walked into the backyard to find me hanging halfway out the window. My three-year-old let him in, and I explained the situation. Even the officer struggled with the baby-proof latch! It took him three tries to open it, but finally, I was free.

Once he took down my info and confirmed I wasn't mentally ill or drunk, we had a good laugh. My toddler, despite locking me in, was officially the hero of the day for his quick thinking and listening skills. And my sleeping baby was none the wiser.

All we could do was laugh.

Because that's motherhood sometimes. It throws you into the most unexpected, crazy situations, and sometimes all you can do is laugh. Laughter in the face of chaos is good for you *and* for your child. That day was a perfect example—you can't make this sh*t up.

Although popular culture is becoming more open about the less-than-glamorous side of mothering, there is still this misconception that it's all cuddles and peaceful sleeping babies and smiling mamas, all picture-perfect moments. But the truth of the situation is that it's often messy and chaotic with situations that almost sound made up because they are so absurd. I have learned to embrace this messy, beautiful chaos and find humor in everything. Life is just so much more enjoyable that way.

Laughter is a welcome release, especially after a stressful situation. Our children look to us to see how we react to situations. If we're calm, they calm down more easily. If we laugh and smile, they often laugh and smile too. This is why you can murmur utter nonsense to your baby with a smile on your face and they react to the joyful inflection in your voice and the positive vibe you are giving out more than they do to your actual words.

So, when you find yourself in one of those stressful moments, remember: laughter can shift the whole vibe and can be a great way to transition out of a "just can't make this sh*t up" situation.

See page 152 for journal prompt.

Day 12:
STAY ON YOUR OWN MAT

When my firstborn started preschool, I signed my youngest up for a Mommy & Me music class. We'd sit in a circle while the leader strummed her guitar, the kids chose from a pile of freshly sterilized instruments, and we all sang and danced. I loved it! I had done something similar with my oldest in our previous town and always looked forward to it.

At first, I looked forward to it with my second child too. It felt like a win-win—my son got to socialize with other kids his age, and I had the chance to be around other moms. Plus singing and dancing are always good for the soul, even the little kid songs.

My son was one of the bolder kids in the class from the start. While many little ones clung to their moms or stayed in their parent's laps, my son would make his way into the center of the circle and dance his little heart out. Everyone laughed, and the attention became fuel for him. As a dancer myself, I loved how much he felt the music.

But about halfway through the 10-week session, things started to shift.

At home, my youngest had started climbing out of his crib—a first for me, since my oldest had never even tried. This made for interrupted nap times, disrupted bedtime routines and a very cranky two-year-old.

Morning routines got harder. He'd fall asleep during the short car ride from drop-off to music class, then arrive cranky and disoriented. He'd perk up, catch a second wind and then get crazy.

What started as dancing a little in the middle turned into running laps around the circle and then running full speed toward the door. I tried to gently corral him back, but it only worked for a few minutes before he'd take off again.

I'd glance around the room and see all the other kids sitting calmly on their parents' laps, wide-eyed with amazement as they watched my wild child zip around. Then I would see the disapproving look of the instructor at my son's manic expression as he ran faster, and it started to feel like the walls were closing in. I would break a sweat chasing him around the room, trying to keep it together, and honestly, it just wasn't fun anymore.

So one day, I left. I scooped up my son, walked out the door and never went back.

Now, I'm not suggesting you abandon every class the moment your child acts up. But in that moment, I realized that music class wasn't the right fit for us anymore.

There's an expression in yoga that's always stuck with me:

"Stay on your own mat."

One of the things that I love most about yoga is that it's very much about honoring your own body, going only as far as what works for you and ultimately not comparing yourself to others or looking around to see who's stretching deeper or holding a pose longer. It's about tuning into your own needs and letting go of comparison.

Whatever shame and frustration I was feeling in that music class was due to my comparing my son to the other more mild-mannered children in the class and also to my older son who used to participate in our other music class in a more orderly fashion.

And, of course, there was the judgment. The instructor's disapproving looks made it clear that she had no understanding of a spirited two-year-old boy's energy levels.

By removing us from the class, I gave into that pressure but I also found a gym class for us that was more suited to my son's state of mind at the time. He absolutely thrived in the gym class, finally in a situation where he could be free to get all his energy out without judgment.

The bottom line is, you can't compare your child to other kids, not even to their own siblings. Each child is unique, with their own personalities, energy levels and ways of experiencing the world. And as parents, we have to remember that we're unique too.

I also had to realize that I was comparing myself too. Why couldn't I control my child like the mom next to me whose child was calmly sitting on her lap? Why do these other moms get to chill and enjoy the music while I am running around trying to catch my very fast two-year-old while also trying not to disrupt the whole class?

So I learned to stay on my own mat—to believe in my child and myself as a mom and redirect accordingly. If something is not working for you or your child, change it. No comparison or judgment needed.

Sometimes that means staying put and adjusting. And sometimes it means picking up your mat and walking out the door. Either way, it's about doing what's best for you and your child.

So, stay on your mat. And if needed, pick up your mat and move it somewhere that feels better.

Namaste.

See page 154 for journal prompt.

Day 13:
REMEMBER THAT YOU ARE
THE SUN AND THE MOON

A few years ago, I had to have major surgery. Surgery is never ideal, but especially not when you have very young children. Still, health comes first. Despite my best intentions, it felt like our house turned upside down. Laundry piled up, the house was a mess and my boys were losing it on a daily basis. I reassured them over and over that I was going to be just fine as they piled into my bed each night for their bedtime stories and gentle hugs and kisses.

But even with my reassurances, they were struggling. Little things sparked big emotions, and they were melting down more easily than usual. With me "down for the count," their little worlds felt like they were crumbling. I'm a constant in their lives, the person they count on. And when I wasn't there to meet their needs, they started to unravel.

I'm sure they were worried too, even if they couldn't put those feelings into words. Kids often forget that parents are people too—

we get sick, we break down, and sometimes, we have to have surgery. Even our babies, who can't possibly understand what sickness or surgery means, can still feel the shift when we're not our best.

Thankfully, after a few weeks, I started getting better. And as I started to feel like myself again, so did they. That's when the realization hit me that, as their mom, I was the sun and the moon to them in these early years. If I go dark, they lose their way.

At times, that can feel like a heavy weight, and I've often felt the pressure of it. But during my recovery, I realized that it's also an honor. For this brief season of their childhood, I hold such a crucial role. I need to be there for them, but not just physically. I need to show up as my best self—emotionally, mentally and spiritually.

How we show up and care for ourselves directly affects how we care for our children. We can't pour from an empty cup. The fuller we are, the more we have to give. The healthier we are, the more present we can be. So the next time you find yourself sacrificing your own needs for theirs, remember that taking care of yourself is also taking care of them.

And as intense as this season can feel, it can help to remember that this role will not last forever. If we do our job right, our children won't always need us to be their sun and moon. This role is a brief honor, a fleeting bunch of years where we are everything to them. This role will shift with time, they'll grow and become more independent, and we will be free again—and most likely, a little sad too. Remembering this helps me fully appreciate this time I have with them. It reminds me of how beautiful it is to be their everything, and it keeps me focused on taking care of myself so I can take the best care of them.

You are the sun and the moon, Mama. Take care of yourself so you can shine as bright as you can.

See page 156 for journal prompt.

DAY 14: THE HEAL IS REAL

My boys both slept in their own cribs as babies, eventually graduating to toddler beds and then twin beds. Sleep has always been a big priority in our house, and we've stuck to a pretty strict schedule. But around age four, my youngest started waking up in the middle of the night and running into our bed.

At first, I did exactly what all the books tell you to do—walk him back to his own bed. But after countless sleepless nights, I gave up and let him stay in the middle.

As it turns out, this actually works for us. We have a king-sized mattress, so there's plenty of room. Once he's comforted and cozy in the middle, he falls right back to sleep. We've created a routine that feels good. We start his bedtime routine in his room, and then later, my husband or I carry him into our bed before we go to sleep. He gets what he needs most—comfort, security and, of course, sleep!

Despite everyone telling me he's too old for this, or that it'll become a habit we'll regret, it feels right for us. So, we keep doing it.

I think back to when I was a child. If I woke up scared in the middle of the night, I'd run into my mom's room. She'd keep a sleeping bag on the floor next to her bed for me to sleep in. I remember lying there for a while sometimes, still feeling scared and not really comforted. She did what worked for her, and I don't blame her for that. But now, I have the chance to give my child the comfort and safety that I craved as a sleepy little girl and that fills up my heart.

This is part of the beauty of having your own children. You get to be the parent you wished you had! It's an empowering feeling. And it's not about blaming your parents. They did what they thought was best at the time, and that's okay. But now it's your turn.

Maybe there are things from your childhood that you want to carry forward with your own kids. Great! For me, vacations were a big part of my childhood and some of my best memories were made on those trips. That's a tradition I'm continuing for my children, and going away together will always be a priority for us.

And maybe there are things from your childhood that you'd rather change. That's great, too.

Having children forces you to take an honest look at your own childhood. It can be deeply healing for your own inner child to break cycles or change behaviors that didn't serve you. You will be forced to look within and remember how you felt as a child, what you wish you had and what you wish you could have changed. This reflection and personal growth can be incredibly empowering.

Healing doesn't just happen—it's intentional. And sometimes, that healing comes from showing up for your children in ways you wish someone had shown up for you. Just another way that having a child facilitates your own growth as a person. The heal is real.

See page 158 for journal prompt.

DAY 15:
IT'S A JUNGLE OUT THERE
ON THE PLAYGROUND

When my oldest completed his first year of preschool, the school hosted a cute little celebration for all of the students and their families. Afterwards, we said our goodbyes with promises of playground meetups and scheduled playdates over the summer. Later that night, one glimpse at social media showed me that *I* hadn't been invited to the party. *He* hadn't been invited to the party.

They were all there—the women I had smiled at and chatted with every day for nine months. The same moms who had held the door for me as I juggled a stroller and a preschooler, who had stood beside me as we said our morning goodbyes and then watched our kids joyfully run into our arms at pickup, who had met up with me at the park, participated with me in class parties and laughed with me about the silly things our little ones did and said. And now they were all at a party and we were not invited.

I felt like I was 13 years old again. Actually, worse—because at 13, I *was* invited to the party. And now there was *him*. My sweet, innocent little four-year-old, who wasn't invited to his good friend's party.

It wasn't his fault we had moved to town after the other families and missed the first year of preschool. It wasn't his fault that I had felt perfectly comfortable staying on the perimeter of that mom group because I already had a tight circle of friends and craved deeper conversations than what a few minutes at drop-off and pickup allowed. This mama bear version of being left out by the mean girls left much more to unpack than any teenage drama.

I cried for me. I cried for us. I cried for him.

Things always sting significantly more when it's done to your child than when it's done to you. But in this situation, I was the only one crying. I was devastated for my child that he didn't get to bounce in the bouncy house with all his friends, but he was none the wiser, another reason to be grateful four-year-olds don't have social media. I got myself together and took comfort in the fact that my sweet boy knew nothing of this very basic unkindness.

Here's the thing, the mean girls are still out there—only some of them grew up to be mean moms now.

But don't let this change who you are. You *will* find your mom friends. Don't let one act of unkindness turn you off to the idea of mom friends. For every one mean mom, there are many more kind, exhausted, just-trying-to-get-through-the-day moms. Looking back, I truly believe that slight had very little to do with me.

That was one mom, and maybe she felt safest in her small mom bubble. Maybe the moms who were invited were too insecure in their own social standing to stick their necks out. Maybe they were just too consumed with surviving motherhood to even notice that some of us were left out. Or maybe they just didn't like me.

Either way, it's all very similar to high school, and the same wisdom applies: *What other people think of you is none of your business.*

Please don't let playground drama get to you. You will find the right mom friends when the time is right. And maybe heal some high school wounds while you are at it.

This is also a chance to be that one kind mom to someone else. Keep your circle open, be kind and be the kind of friend you want your child to have.

Just another way that having kids helps you heal your past and makes you a better person.

See page 160 for journal prompt.

DAY 16:
FIND SOMETHING NEW

When my first baby was four months old, I was walking through our new neighborhood (we seem to move every time I'm pregnant) when I stopped to chat with another mom pushing a stroller. She lived just a block down and noticed the book tucked under my stroller. I shared how, when my baby fell asleep in the park, I'd sometimes stop, sit on a bench and read for a bit. I also mentioned that I used to belong to a book club in my former city, back before I became a mom. She smiled and said, "We should start one here!"

And so, we did.

We became a group of seven moms, all avid readers, all living within a quarter mile of each other. We met once a month at a different member's house, sharing food, enjoying a glass of wine, commiserating about motherhood and yes, actually talking about the book! I came to treasure these monthly gatherings. They became a lifeline for me.

The book club was social, therapeutic and, most importantly, convenient. Meetings started after I put my baby down for the night and once my husband was home from work, so it fit seamlessly into my routine. It also motivated me to finish the selected book each month so I could contribute to the discussion. One book a month, squeezed in during naps or at the park, felt totally doable, and I appreciated the nudge to make time for it. That book club gave me exactly what I needed during that season of life. It showed me that even when things feel overwhelming, adding just one simple thing can make it all feel so much better.

So much of motherhood, especially in the early days, is routine, routine, routine. And that's a good thing—life feels a little easier once you survive those first few weeks and settle into a rhythm. You know when the baby eats, sleeps, gets cranky and sleeps again. You know when it's time to take the baby for a walk, to clean, to rest. And with every new change, the routine shifts again. But no matter how it shifts, it can often feel like rinse and repeat. Routine is orderly and comforting. But it can also make you feel stagnant as if you're living in *Groundhog Day*.

That's why it's so important to shake it up, just a little.

What are you curious about? What's something you've always wanted to learn or try? I'm not talking about backpacking through Europe. I'm talking baby steps, like joining an art class on Tuesday nights, an online nutrition course or a knitting club that meets once a month. Something that fits into your life without taking away from your routine. Something that you can pull off and still show up for your baby and your routine. But something that gets your juices flowing, wakes up your brain, sparks your creativity and reminds you of who you are beyond being a mom.

Even the smallest addition, something that might seem silly or insignificant, can make a world of difference. It can pull you out of that routine comfort zone, give you a fresh breath of air and help you feel like *you* again. It might even help you discover a whole new side of yourself.

And if it feels overwhelming, it's not the right choice. Pick something simple, something that fits easily into your schedule and feels joyful. Sometimes the smallest change is all it takes to shift your mindset and remind you that you count too. Because you do!

See page 162 for journal prompt.

DAY 17: BRINGING SEXY BACK

When my firstborn was three months old, my maternity photographer's partner was offering a deal on boudoir sessions. Basically, it's a photo shoot where you have your hair and makeup done, dress up in sexy outfits and walk away with a collection of photos of yourself. I figured it would be something fun, and I liked the idea of having a little extra motivation to tone up my body again. We scheduled it for two months later.

As the date approached, I heard this voice in my head saying, *Maybe I should just cancel,* or *Do I really need the extra stress of trying to look sexy right now? I'm a mom. Moms aren't supposed to be sexy.*

But I had already given a deposit and picked out my outfits, so I thought, *why not?*

I had no idea how empowering it would be.

First, it was really fun! It felt great to sip a glass of champagne while someone else did my hair and makeup with fun music playing in the background. And much to the photographer's credit, she made me feel so comfortable and confident. It turned into an amazing afternoon, where I focused on myself, had some fun and remembered that I am still a woman, even though I'm now a mom.

Boudoir sessions can be done at any time, and while it might seem like an odd choice just five months after childbirth, for me, it was perfect. During pregnancy, our bodies are constantly being observed, poked and prodded. It's a beautiful experience to grow a life inside you, but it can also make you feel a bit like a piece of meat or just a vessel to grow another life. Then after the baby is born, we are left recovering and still giving our body to someone else. It's part of the miracle of motherhood, but somewhere in all of that giving, it's easy to forget that there's still a woman in there too.

That photo shoot gave me back my power, not just as a mom, but as a woman. As a sexual being who owns her body. I'm not just a babymaker. My body was made for other things too. And also, post-birth bodies are sexy!

And here's the thing, all of these benefits happened before I even saw the pictures. Because it wasn't just about how I looked, but how I felt. I am so proud of my body. I mean, I grew an actual human being in there. Just for a second, stop and think about how incredible that is! The female body is beautiful, powerful, strong and sexy, and it deserves to be celebrated. The boudoir session gave me the space to put my baby lovingly down for a few hours and simply be that woman.

And when I finally saw the photos, I was even more impressed.

It felt so good to see myself through the lens of the camera and not just through my own critical mind. As women, we often don't give ourselves the recognition we deserve for how beautiful we are. We think we need to be perfect to be radiant, but we don't. These photos, so out of the ordinary for me, allowed me to see myself almost as if I was looking at someone else.

What started as a gift for my husband became an unexpected gift for me too.

I strongly encourage you to consider a boudoir shoot for yourself. It can be a motivator if you're working toward becoming stronger or returning to your pre-baby body. Or it can be a beautiful way to celebrate your curves and capture this season of life, baby weight and all. Most importantly, it can really help you feel empowered again in your own body and celebrate yourself as a sexual being and as a woman.

The most important part is feeling comfortable with the photographer and the setting. That's why I chose a female photographer I trusted, and a location that I knew well and where I felt safe. Once those pieces are in place, it's okay to feel a little out of your comfort zone. That's where the magic happens.

Bring your sexy back—you might just surprise yourself.

See page 164 for journal prompt.

DAY 18: TIME IS ON YOUR SIDE

When my older son was two, my second son was born. My husband took two weeks off to stay home as we adjusted to life as a family of four. And then he went back to work. His job in New York City meant he left early in the morning to catch a train and didn't return until long after our older son had gone to bed. Those were some of the longest days of my life. What had already felt overwhelming with him home now felt even more so with him gone.

Every weekend, we were two again. I was still doing a lot, but it wasn't all on my shoulders like it was during the week. And every Sunday night, I would feel the anxiety begin to creep in—the impending week looming like a dark cloud. That's when I learned to break time into smaller pieces.

Instead of thinking about the entire week ahead, I began to focus only on the next day. On Sunday night, I would look at Monday. On Monday night, I looked at Tuesday. And so on. If I could get through one more day, then I could get through one more day again and again. But sometimes, even that felt overwhelming. So

I broke it down further—one hour at a time, one nap at a time. If I could just make it until the morning nap, then the afternoon nap, then bedtime. Whatever got me through.

Those first few months of juggling a baby and a toddler were intense. But like a long hike up a mountain, breaking it into smaller stretches made it feel less overwhelming.

Much like running a marathon, if you fixate on the full 26.2 miles, it can feel overwhelming—impossible, even. But if you just focus on the next mile, then the next, and the next, the impossible becomes possible. And don't forget to look back. Take in the full 26.2 miles behind you. See how far you've come, how many miles you've already run, and give yourself a pat on the back.

You are stronger than you think and capable of more than you know. Break it up as you move forward but always take a moment to look back and celebrate how far you've come.

See page 166 for journal prompt.

DAY 19: GRATITUDE WORKS!

I discovered the book *The Magic* a year before I became a mom, and I dove right in. It's a 28-day gratitude practice book, and it is amazing. First, you're asked to list everything you truly want in life and get very, very clear on it. Then, you follow the practice for 28 days straight, completing a different activity each day. One constant throughout the 28 days, in addition to the daily task, is making a list of 10 things you are grateful for and why. I really felt this practice opened a lot of doors for me and changed my perspective on life. From there on, I gobbled up anything I could on gratitude and have found ways to tailor it to every phase of my life.

One practice in particular has stuck with me, and I still find myself using it whenever I need to pull myself out of the drudgery of everyday life. It's a simple shift: approaching your day as a series of "get to" moments instead of "have to" moments. This one is especially relevant for motherhood. Each day, I would wake up to my baby crying or cooing—I "get to" see my baby every morning, instead of thinking, "I have to get up now." I "get to" nourish my baby instead of feeling like I "have to" feed my baby. I "get to" be the one he cries for and the one who soothes him, instead of thinking, "I have to" always be the one to pick him up. This simple change in perspective was a game-changer for me and really helped me through those endless-feeling days—especially the times when I felt resentful, overtouched or completely exhausted.

I also created my own "three-a-day" rule. In those early years of motherhood and overwhelm, writing a list of 10 things I was grateful for felt like too much. Instead, each morning while feeding my son or each night while rocking him to sleep, I would list three things in my head that I was grateful for. The beauty of this is that it requires no pen and paper, no extra time set aside—it's just in your head. And if there's one thing you have now, it's time in your own thoughts.

Even on the hardest, most exhausting days, I never had to search too far to find three things to be grateful for.

> *I am so thankful for the lovely afternoon nap my son took today that gave me a quiet moment to read.*

> *I am so happy and grateful for the most delicious Chinese food tonight—it tasted great, and I didn't have to cook!*

> *Thank you, thank you, thank you for a clean bill of health at my son's checkup today. How lucky am I to have such a healthy child?*

Each day, I found more and more to appreciate. Sometimes, I would even say my gratitude out loud to my baby. It's never too early to instill a positive outlook in your child, and babies love nothing more than the sound of their mother's voice, especially when it's filled with gratitude.

Now is a great time to begin a gratitude practice. Simply shifting "have to" to "get to" and practicing the three-a-day rule in your head can be incredibly powerful. These are gentle, easy shifts to make, and the more you use them, the more natural they become. The beauty of gratitude is that the more you practice it, the more things you attract into your life to be grateful for. Gratitude is a gift and an essential tool for the long days of motherhood and, let's be honest, for life in general.

Thank you, thank you, thank you!

See page 168 for journal prompt.

DAY 20: THE MISSING PIECE

On Christmas Day each year, we stay home, just the four of us. This was a tradition we started when both of our boys were babies. We wake up on Christmas morning, open our gifts, have brunch and then stay in pajamas all day, playing with new toys and simply enjoying being home. The day after Christmas, and throughout the holiday break, we make the rounds to see extended family.

One Christmas morning, I received a 1,000-piece puzzle as a gift. While the boys played with their toys, I started working on my puzzle. I spent the entire day moving in and out of the zone, completely absorbed in it. Then, over the next few nights, I found myself glued to it. It was incredibly satisfying to put my undivided energy into something—and then actually finish it!

That's when I realized how much of my daily life with small children consisted of things that were never quite done. Laundry, cleaning up, emptying the dishwasher, changing diapers—each task was completed only to be repeated again and again. It was an endless cycle, a never-ending merry-go-round.

That puzzle over Christmas break gave me an unexpected sense of completion and satisfaction, something I didn't even realize I was missing. And it sounds so silly. Who cares if I finish a puzzle? Nobody but me. But maybe that was the point. There was no purpose to finishing it for anyone but myself. No award to be won, nobody's life changed or even affected. This was all for me.

What feeling are you missing? The ability to turn your full attention to something other than your children? The satisfaction of completing something? The stimulation of using your brain in a different way? Adult interaction? Feeling useful? Identify what's missing for you at this moment and find a way to fulfill it.

This doesn't have to be something big or dramatic. You don't even have to tell anyone about it. If something as simple as a puzzle could fulfill my need to complete something, then there are simple solutions for the other missing pieces, too. There are so many small things you can add to your day once you pinpoint what's missing for you. And the answer may change from day to day or phase to phase. But you may surprise yourself with what comes up just by taking the time to ask the question. Sometimes, you don't even realize what you truly need until it's missing from your life.

When you feel completely overwhelmed, adding something else to your plate may seem counterintuitive. You might feel like you can't possibly handle one more thing, but believe it or not, adding one small thing can actually help restore a sense of balance to your life.

Completing a crossword puzzle, having an uninterrupted phone conversation with your best friend, enjoying a quiet meal with a nice glass of wine—just adults, no distractions. The possibilities are endless.

So, what feeling are you missing?

See page 170 for journal prompt.

DAY 21: LAUGH, CRY, RINSE, REPEAT

When my little one was two, he started climbing out of the crib, thus beginning one of my hardest chapters of motherhood. My oldest was finally in preschool for three hours a day, and that time had perfectly coincided with my little one's naptime. But the crib escape stole this time from me like a thief in the night.

Now, our mornings consisted of waking up, having breakfast, getting ready for preschool and wrangling my littlest out of the car to walk my four-year-old inside. Then, I'd wrangle my little one back into the car and hit the Starbucks drive-thru. After that, I'd drive around, sipping my coffee and praying he'd fall asleep, because this was the only way he would nap. By that point, he was fighting the stroller so hard that a walk was out of the question, and his crib had become a jungle gym. So, driving around it was!

And that blissful moment when he finally fell asleep brought me a rare, peaceful coffee experience as I kept driving. But I had to keep moving—anytime I stopped for too long, he would startle awake.

Most days, this was the moment my exhausted guard finally dropped as I'd been holding it together all morning—with no distractions in the car, the tears would start to fall. It was as if, in that quiet space, I could finally feel my exhaustion and stress and release into a puddle. And really, what better time to do so? These were my only moments of the day completely alone—no one asking me questions, no chores to distract me— just the car, some music, a sleeping two-year-old and a cup of coffee.

Crying is a release. Whether it's from physical pain, frustration, exhaustion, sadness or relief, tears are our body's way of processing overwhelming emotions. Unreleased emotions don't just disappear, they explode later, or worse, they get stored in our bodies and physically manifest in other ways. Crying is a way to regulate and let emotions flow, just like laughter.

I always felt better after my tearful joyrides. By the time my youngest awoke from his nap and we went to pick up my older son, I felt lighter. Not more rested, by any means, but free from the heavy emotions that had weighed me down just hours earlier.

In the depths of motherhood—when hormones are out of whack and sleep is hard to come by, there are bound to be tears. Let them come. Let them out. Release what you can. Choosing your moments strategically can help you avoid a complete breakdown in front of your children. And the beautiful thing is that once the tears have paved the way, laughter often follows. Often, once I had my cry and I felt lighter, I was able to be more present with my children, more playful, and the laughter just flowed.

Laughter is also a release of emotions, and there's a reason why tears and laughter so often go hand in hand. Crying clears space, and laughter fills it with connection and joy. Motherhood presents so many ridiculous moments when you can either laugh or cry. Take the time to release the tears so you can turn to laughter when it counts. Your little ones are watching you closely, and they will delight in hearing your laughter. Plus, it's contagious—and there's no better sound in the world than your child laughing, especially when you're doing it together. Pro tip: Always keep a box of tissues in the car!

See page 172 for journal prompt.

Day 22:
ANGELS ARE ALL AROUND

When my little one was a baby, I would take him and my three-year-old grocery shopping every week. It gave us an outing, and we needed groceries so: win-win! I'd strap my baby into the carrier on my chest and sit my three-year-old in the front of the cart. They loved it, and over time, we found a nice rhythm gathering the groceries we needed for the week.

The hardest part was loading the groceries into the car, getting the kids strapped into their car seats and returning the cart. There was just no way to do it gracefully, and I never wanted to leave them unattended in a busy parking lot.

One day, I loaded the groceries into the trunk with my baby still strapped to my chest, one foot keeping the cart (with my three-year-old in it) from rolling away, as I always did. A woman approached us with a warm smile and said, "Can I please take this cart off your hands? I need one anyway." Gratefully, I accepted her offer. As I lifted my three-year-old out of the cart and into his seat, she walked away with the cart, and I got the baby into his seat.

But as I got into the driver's seat, ready to pull out, I noticed something. The woman who had approached us was now getting into her car to leave. She hadn't needed a grocery cart at all. She had simply seen a tired, stressed-looking mom and stepped in to help by returning my cart.

Angels don't always have wings. Sometimes, they're just ordinary people who see a need and offer a helping hand. Maybe this woman had been in my shoes before, struggling with little kids in a parking lot. Or maybe she was simply a kind person.

If you're open to them, angels are everywhere. And now, I find myself eagerly accepting the opportunities I see to be an angel for someone else.

Watch for the angels. I guarantee the more you notice them, the more they appear!

See page 174 for journal prompt.

Day 23: PICK YOUR POISON

When I was first home with my baby, I thought I would have so much free time. All babies do is eat and sleep, right? My firstborn loved to be held all the time, while he was eating and while he was sleeping. And I was happy to keep my arms full, happy to be the one to soothe him.

Once we found our groove and I could actually put him down for naps and bedtime, I found myself with some time with my arms empty.

Personally, I was never someone who could "sleep when the baby sleeps." By then, I had mastered the art of fueling myself with caffeine, and I often used naptime or bedtime as a chance to clean up, do laundry and cook dinner. Along with the "sleep when the baby sleeps" advice came the classic "leave the mess" advice. But for me, that was never an option. I personally feel more stressed when my house is a mess. Motherhood brings enough chaos without my environment adding to it. When my house is in order,

I feel calmer. Even on the days I felt utterly exhausted, I couldn't fully rest until I had cleaned up and everything felt orderly again.

Once I had a solid nap and sleep schedule, I built a cleaning schedule too. It was worth it to me to do one cleaning sweep and maybe some dinner prep right after I put my baby down for his afternoon nap. That way, I could use the rest of naptime for something I actually wanted to do—a quick workout, a cup of tea with my book or one of those 20–minute breaks I swear by. Then, once he was down, I'd clean up again, but it was much less because I had already done the afternoon reset. This system worked for me.

Maybe you're the same, and a clean house makes you feel calm. Or maybe you can take the "leave the mess" advice to heart, choosing to rest or do something else that brings you joy instead. The key here is finding what works for you. What makes you feel calm and in control? What are your non-negotiables? For me, I couldn't fall asleep knowing there was a big mess waiting for me in the morning. Maybe that's not the case for you. Maybe you have a partner who comes home at night and picks up the slack. Maybe you know that if you spend naptime cleaning, you'll feel more stressed and resentful when your baby wakes up. If that's the case, then naptime might be better spent doing something just for yourself or, like me, a combination of both.

This isn't about following a one-size-fits-all piece of advice. It's about getting to know yourself.

What I also learned about myself is that I have "production windows"—times of the day when I have the most energy. I know that after my first cup of coffee in the morning, I have the most energy, so moving around during that window is essential. But that also happens to be the time my baby refused to nap in the crib and just wanted to be close to me. So, we made that our favorite time for a walk. I got to move, my baby got to be close to me, and sometimes he'd drift off a little or just listen to me talk or sing as we walked. Then, in the afternoon, when my energy was lower, I'd fit in a meditation, some reading or rest (after my quick cleaning sweep, of course).

The most important thing is to find what works for you and your children. Maybe you have more energy at night and prefer to clean up after you put the baby down for the night so you're set up for tomorrow. Or maybe you love waking up early, getting things done before your kids are up and using naptime for a nap for yourself.

You get to set the schedule. Or maybe your baby sets the schedule, and you work around it. Either way, there is no one-size-fits-all routine that works for everyone.

Try letting go of what you think you "should" be doing in the moment and just own it. This is your life, your baby and your time. If mess doesn't stress you out, leave it! If you'd rather rest than cook dinner, order in! If your idea of resting is catching up on your shows during naptime, have at it!

Once you know yourself, you can find what works for you and do it with intention. Give yourself rest, give yourself breaks, and don't spend your time doing something while thinking you "should" be doing something else. You are in charge, and you need to do what works in your home, not anyone else's.

Pick your poison and trust yourself.

See page 176 for journal prompt.

DAY 24: NOURISH YOURSELF

I was so excited when my first baby was ready to try orange foods. I carefully picked out organic sweet potatoes, steamed them, pureed them and watched as he happily gobbled down his first bite. An hour later, it was my turn for dinner, and I grabbed a protein bar because I just didn't feel like cooking.

In that moment, it hit me—I was honoring my baby's body, but I wasn't honoring my own.

From the moment we find out we're pregnant, we're given a long list of what we should and shouldn't eat—no sushi, no alcohol, no deli meat and, the first time I was pregnant, even no cantaloupe because of a listeria recall. Why then, as soon as the baby is born, does all the focus shift to nourishing them, without much concern for us mamas? Sure, if you're breastfeeding, there are still some dos and don'ts, but whether you nurse or not, you are still healing. You need energy to survive the crazy newborn phase on little sleep, and you matter, too.

This isn't about losing baby weight or getting back to a certain size; you already have enough stress keeping another little human alive. This is about nourishing yourself, fueling your body and treating it with the same care and value as your baby's. Postpartum hormones are all over the place, and the combination of sleep deprivation and stress can send your cortisol levels soaring. Reaching for fast food, sugar and too much caffeine might feel like the easy fix, but it can actually make things worse. Now is the time for healing, delicious nutrient-dense foods that comfort both your body and soul. I know it sounds easier said than done when you barely have time to shower, let alone cook, but it's worth it.

And it doesn't have to be a big production. Before I had kids, I used to mock crock pots, but during the infant stage, my slow cooker became my best friend. You can make simple, healthy wholesome meals with barely any effort—soups, stews, chili, even plain shredded chicken for easy meals. The key is to find what works for you, foods that make you feel nourished and cared for while keeping your body fueled and your blood sugar balanced. Once you have a few go-to recipes that you love, put them on rotation, make big batches so you have leftovers and call it a day.

The same goes for coffee and tea. I love my morning coffee, but if I overdo it, I get jittery and my stomach hurts. Find the right amount of caffeine that works for you and add in a matcha latte or some soothing herbal tea for comfort without excess caffeine.

This isn't about restriction or dieting. Treat yourself to takeout sometimes, focus on whole foods most of the time and gather a few easy, nourishing recipes to keep in your routine. Treat yourself with the same care you give your baby, and you'll heal faster, feel better, and have the energy to be the best mom you can be. Remember, you matter, too.

This is also a great time to take a closer look at your vices. Mom culture is full of wine jokes and merch labeled "mommy juice." But it's important to decide what actually works for you. When my second was less than a year old and we were in the middle of moving, I treated myself to one glass of red wine every night after the kids were in bed. I looked forward to that one glass all day and I enjoyed it with dinner, so it didn't affect how I felt the next day. It was a ritual that helped me unwind. But over time, I realized I felt better without it. After that stressful phase, I started saving wine for nights out or special occasions because I realized that I felt my best without it. I found other ways to relax, like a hot shower or getting in bed with a book. If a glass of wine helps you decompress, go for it.

However, if you find that you feel out of control with your alcohol intake or if it's affecting your sleep, your energy or your overall well-being, it might be worth reconsidering it as a way to unwind. The point is to be honest with yourself about what you need right now and possibly examine any vices that may not be serving you. Take care of yourself in a way that makes you feel your best, not just for your baby, but for you. Because how you feel matters, too.

See page 178 for journal prompt.

DAY 25: SHOW YOUR CARDS

When my firstborn was two, we started a Mommy & Me gym class. It gave him a much-needed outlet to run around, and it gave me a chance to connect with other moms. I was excited to finally be around other kids and parents again after what had been a long winter without much social interaction for either of us.

In between chasing our toddlers, the moms would all chat about sleep schedules, pacifiers and who was talking yet. Every time someone asked how anyone was doing, the answers were always the same: "Great." "Good." "Well." Smiles all around.

Okay, I thought, *maybe it's just me who's struggling a bit. Maybe I can learn from these moms how to be "great" every day.*

And then, one day, after a rough night of my son going through a sleep regression, I just didn't have it in me to pretend that I was "great." After the usual chorus of "How are you?" "Great!" "Good!" "Well!" circled around to me, I said, "Not so great. We barely slept last night, and now he won't nap because he's overtired. I'm just so exhausted." Then I started to cry a little, mostly from sheer exhaustion.

Immediately, most of the women let down their guard and let it out. One mom said she'd also been up most of the night. One mom was on her third cup of coffee and still barely functioning, another was also up most of the night too. And on it went. I'll never forget one mom, the one who was always "great," trying to manage her usual smile, then just walking away. She just wasn't ready to go there. And that's okay, too.

What I learned that day is this: if you think you're the only one struggling, you're not. You are never alone. I'm not saying every gathering needs to become a complaint fest, but we have to stop pretending everything is "great" when it's not. Because when you're brave enough to be honest and vulnerable, you open the door for others to be honest, too. And even if they happen to be "great" that day, they'll be able to relate because they've been there.

Motherhood can be a lonely place. But it doesn't have to be. It can also be a beautiful time of deep connection and bonding for women. It can be a space where all feelings are welcome, and sharing the pain can help us heal.

Toxic positivity is real. And while I'm all for making the best in a situation when you can, sometimes you just need to let it out. And the beauty of letting it out is that you can also help someone else feel less alone.

Some moms refuse to go there and some just can't. And that's okay. You'll find your people. You'll find your safe spaces, and you'll also be able to create safe spaces for other moms. But it all starts with honesty, with not pretending. And it can start with you.

I walked out of that gym class still exhausted—but lighter, happier and just a little bit healed, and I would like to think that the other moms did too. That class became a lifeline for me, a weekly reminder that I wasn't alone. By the time my second child came along, I skipped the pretending altogether, and I found my lifelines more quickly. I've also had the chance to be a lifeline, too, especially for first-time moms who I can just tell are pretending. They need it the most.

And maybe you do, too.

See page 180 for journal prompt.

DAY 26: EMBRACE THE SOUL YOU ARE RAISING

One morning, I was getting my son ready for school and we were running late. We barely got out the door when I realized I had forgotten my handbag. I ran back inside to get it, and when I came back out, my son was crouched down on the ground with his hands covered in dirt. Right away, the words came out before I had a chance to process: "What are you doing? Put those worms down! You can't go to school with worm germs on your hands!" I quickly got his hands washed and got him off to school.

Only later did I realize what he had been doing.

The words he had said right before heading to school hung in the air: "But I have to save them." It had rained the night before, and our driveway was now home to many worms, washed out of their homes and awaiting certain death as the sun baked the blacktop. My sweet boy was trying to return them to the grass and save them. And rather than stop and celebrate this little boy with a heart of gold, I had scolded him for getting his hands dirty. I was more concerned with hygiene and what others would say if my son arrived at school with dirty hands than I was with taking in the beauty of this kind animal-loving soul right in front of me.

Our kids are only ours for such a short time. And in that time, we get glimpses of who they really are—what lights them up and what they are put on this earth to do. We can guide them and teach them, but I truly believe they arrive here with personalities all their own. Now, I love animals too and I would never kill a fly, but I would not be down in the dirt saving the worms. But my son is. And in that moment, his nature-loving side was out in full glory. From the time he could crawl, he had a gentle way about him and a profound respect for animals and insects. In hindsight, I admire his strong conviction to do the right thing, even if it meant getting yelled at by his mom for getting his hands dirty.

As our kids grow up, society, friends, media and life in general all have a way of taking the little sparks that make up our kids and extinguishing them, leaving darkness where there was once light. I want to keep those sparks alive for as long as I can, and I certainly don't want to be the one who puts them out before they have a chance to burn.

So much advice thrown at moms is to "not blink," but that feels overwhelming and utterly impossible when you're in survival mode. That's not my advice. That advice is a luxury only those who have already come out of the weeds can give. But what I will say is this: try not to miss too many glimpses. You get the best seats in the house to the little soul growing up before you. And while they are young, those glimpses are pure—a direct line to who they really are, whether it's similar to you or not. So take in those little sparks when you see them, appreciate them and nourish them so they can grow. These little souls are who they are, and the best we can do is let them be exactly that for as long as we can—and enjoy the show.

Spoiler alert: it's a beautiful performance!

See page 182 for journal prompt.

DAY 27: SURRENDER

One Thanksgiving in the middle of dinner, my son came down with a fever. My initial thought was for his well-being, of course, but then came the intrusive, controlling thoughts. What if we just infected everyone around my mom's table for the holiday? What if my whole family, plus the random guy my cousin brought, gets sick now? (Just kidding, there was no random guy, but still... crazy thoughts!) How will we drive the three hours home with a nauseous kid? What about my younger son's best friend's birthday party in two days that he's been so excited to attend? What about my husband's board meeting on Monday? What if I also get super sick, and then my husband goes back to work, and I can't take care of anyone?

Who is this person spinning out in my head? Before I became a mom, the "what ifs" didn't even occur to me most of the time. Motherhood changed that—and the sheer responsibility of two little lives, plus all the unexpected things that pop up, put me on shaky ground.

That Thanksgiving, I quickly got my son set up in the guest room, rubbed his back, took his temperature and made sure he was comfortable. Then I realized something important—I had just done everything within my control. Everything else? Completely out of my control. I had no choice but to surrender. Sometimes that can be enough.

But when it's not, or when the intrusive thoughts don't quiet down, I have learned to consider the positive "what ifs" and to lean into them. What if this is just a one-day bug and he wakes up totally fine tomorrow? What if everyone else is completely fine and nobody gets sick? What if everything just works out? Surrender.

There is so much beauty in the surrender. There is power there. A release of sorts. There's freedom in knowing—and accepting—that so much is outside of our control. Motherhood will throw you for some loops for sure, but it's all part of the ride. Worrying about every little thing that could possibly go wrong might give you a false sense of control, but that's all it is—false. There is no controlling everything. There is so much out of your hands, and yes, that can feel scary, but I promise that acknowledging that it's out of your hands can also be incredibly freeing.

And even outside of motherhood, in our everyday lives, what would happen if we just let go and stopped holding on so tightly? What if we released the things outside of our power, let go of the useless worry over what may or may not happen and saved our energy for what we *can* do in the now? Maybe even enjoy the ambiguity of what's unfolding.

Motherhood is a great practice in letting go. That practice can easily spill into how we handle the rest of life, too. Enjoy the sweet surrender.

See page 184 for journal prompt.

DAY 28: BOUNDARIES, BOUNDARIES, BOUNDARIES!

When my first baby was a few weeks old, it was the start of flu season, and my husband and I mostly stayed home with him. We would go for walks around the neighborhood or spend time outside in our backyard, but for the most part, we avoided public places and kept visitors to a minimum.

One close relative in particular was coming to visit after already meeting him in the hospital right after he was born. This relative was the only visitor we had coming who smoked cigarettes. I had been around this person while I was pregnant and tried to respectfully keep my distance while they were smoking, too polite to make a direct request for space. Then, in the hospital, I was too distracted by childbirth, the blissful relief from pain and the intoxicating new baby smell to worry about possible smoke exposure. But now that I was a few weeks in, there was no denying the fact that I was 100 percent uncomfortable with someone who smelled of smoke holding my baby. Luckily, my husband felt the same way, so we were on the same page.

Since it was my husband's family member, I left it to him to have a chat. His request was met with pushback, and an argument about the effects of secondhand smoke on newborns ensued. Have babies of previous generations survived smoke exposure? Absolutely. Did women used to smoke while pregnant and probably while nursing? Most definitely. But when you know better, you do better. Also, none of those facts actually mattered.

What mattered is that we, as the newborn parents, got to make the rules. Period.

I had been uncomfortable many times while pregnant—having this person speaking close to me while smoking—but I still maintained a level of politeness, caring more about hurting the other person's feelings than protecting myself. But this amazing shift happened after I actually had my baby.

As his mom, I just had this knowing. I knew that smoke exposure was not good for his little lungs, and every bone in my body told me to protect him from that. It didn't mean this person couldn't come into our home, but clean hands and smoke-free clothing were nonnegotiable if they wanted to pick up and hold my baby. And I cared about my baby more than I cared about someone else being offended. That clarity felt extremely empowering.

The amazing thing is, with each knowing, more and more came. And the more I practiced exercising these boundaries, the stronger I felt, and the easier it became to set and hold them. You may not have all the answers when it comes to raising and protecting your baby or children, but as their mom, you also have that knowing deep inside. So when you feel it, listen to it. Don't ignore that little gift. Biologically, we are linked to our babies in a way nobody else is, and the more you trust yourself, the more you'll be able to set boundaries and stick up for yourself and your beliefs—even when there is pushback. *Especially* when there is pushback. The people who fight you on your boundaries or try to talk you out of them are often the very people you need to set those boundaries with the most.

You don't have to convince anyone or overexplain. You can lovingly set the boundary and let them decide whether they're willing to follow it. You are not asking for permission. The other person doesn't have to agree with the boundary—but if they want to be around your child, they do have to respect it. Remember: your child, your rules.

Setting boundaries at first may feel extremely uncomfortable, especially if you're like I was and used to putting other people's feelings ahead of your own. But remember—a boundary is not a wall; it's a bridge. It's a clear, loving way to invite people into your life and your child's. You're not pushing others away—you're protecting your peace and your child's well-being.

This is your baby, your children. You are in charge. And the more you prioritize what's best for them over what makes other people comfortable, the stronger a mother you will become.

The beautiful part is that, like everything else we've talked about here, this trickles into life outside of motherhood too. Pay attention to how you feel around other people. Some don't have your best interest at heart. Some suck your energy dry. Some give you anxiety just by being in the room. Pay attention to those feelings. Listen for the knowing. Take advantage of the increased sensitivity that often comes with becoming a mom—set your mom boundaries and then keep going. Carry them into every part of your life.

Becoming a mom is an excellent opportunity to learn how to set boundaries in your own life. And if someone fights you hard on a healthy boundary, remember—that's proof you really needed one with that person in the first place.

Boundaries are a healthy expression of self-respect and self-awareness. They are a powerful tool to help ensure that you're surrounding yourself with healthy, supportive relationships, and that's something your kids deserve to see, too.

See page 186 for journal prompt.

DAY 29:
DON'T POOH-POOH THE WOO

The quiet is like a warm cocoon surrounding me. I barely notice someone next to me shifting her position on her mat. The sound of the rain on the windows is almost like music. I am fully comfortable and cozy on my own mat with a blanket draped over me. When was the last time I was this relaxed?

Bong! Bong! The loud sound almost makes me jump, although my body feels so heavy that it can't move. Bong! Bong! This time I am prepared, so it's not as alarming—but still just as loud. My body accepts the sounds, and I feel myself sinking deeper into my mat. The sounds continue.

And then it's over. I am being told to wiggle my fingers and toes and come back into the room. Has it really been a whole hour? Did I drift off? Where did I go? Everyone around me starts to sit up. One woman in the corner is wiping away tears. One man's gentle snoring ends as he, too, starts to move around and open his eyes. The instructor greets us with a smile and assures us that all responses are welcome—and that they'll be different for everyone.

I gently stretch and sit up to gather my things. I feel calm, a little sleepy and very relaxed. I have just experienced my first Himalayan sound bath. I walk out of the yoga studio feeling a little woozy but also with such a sense of calm and peace.

During a Himalayan sound bath, the instructor uses crystal bowls of different sizes to create rhythmic sounds. These sounds activate the parasympathetic nervous system, triggering the release of feel-good chemicals and ultimately creating a sense of peace, calm, relaxation and balance. Or, as I can best describe it— that *everything is going to be okay* feeling.

The best part about it is that you do not have to understand it or even believe in it to experience positive results. In fact, like most of my discoveries with "woo woo" experiences, all you have to do is show up and be a little open to the experience to reap the benefits.

For me, it all began in college with my first yoga class. What started as a way to keep my body toned had such a profound effect on my mental state too. I knew there was something about connecting my breath to movement that felt natural to me. And from there, I have added on restorative yoga, meditation, tai chi, reiki, tapping and, now, Himalayan sound baths. Basically, I will try anything as long as I keep feeling the positive results.

Maybe you have sampled from the woo-woo menu too? If not, being in the weeds is a great time to begin.

Before I became a mom, I was certainly open-minded and curious about energy work and healing and gladly signed up for different experiences. But once I became a mom—and felt the hit my nervous system took from all the hormones and chaos that came with that—I often turned to energy work in a desperate attempt to heal what I couldn't even understand.

Motherhood will bring all kinds of feelings to the surface: feelings from your own childhood, deep-seated emotions, anxiety, worry, sadness and even bliss over becoming responsible for another human life. Motherhood changes you. It is an experience that you will never understand until you live it. So, with uncharted waters come uncharted solutions.

There is no better time to embrace the woo—or at least consider that there may be something else for you to try to regain that "everything will be okay" feeling deep inside. Trying something new and getting out of your comfort zone can get you out of a rut when you feel stuck in the same routine every day. It also carries the added benefit of creating time for yourself and putting yourself first. And if you're like me, you may also learn tools that you can pass down to your children. Both of my boys now have a meditation practice at night as part of their bedtime routines.

This is a beautiful time to be alive, with so many alternative health and wellness options readily available no matter where you live. Local yoga studios, wellness centers, online resources and meditation and tapping apps are literally right at your fingertips.

So, take a chance and stay open-minded to everything and anything that can help you restore your balance. Because remember, the more you can create peace within yourself, the more you can pass down that same feeling to your child. It starts with you. Don't pooh-pooh the woo.

Namaste.

See page 188 for journal prompt.

DAY 30: FORGIVE YOURSELF AGAIN AND AGAIN

One rainy Tuesday, when my boys were one and three, we were stuck in the house all day. My youngest wasn't feeling well, and my oldest was full of energy. I felt like a ping pong ball, bouncing back and forth between the two of them. One minute we were building block towers, the next we were snuggled up reading books. I was doing my best to be there for both of them, but the more stretched I felt, the more each of them seemed to need me. There just wasn't enough of me to go around.

Finally, afternoon nap time arrived and I got my little one down successfully. He was all stuffy and hadn't slept well the night before, and because he was overtired, he fussed through his morning nap—which would have been the one chance for the one-on-one time my oldest was craving. I gave up on that nap and kept going, still ping-ponging between the two, trying to mask my growing frustration.

By the time afternoon rolled around, I was done. My baby was finally asleep, and I was taking my time with my oldest's nap routine, trying desperately to be present and give him undivided attention, while also desperately wishing he would just fall asleep so I could have one hour of quiet.

He was probably feeling my urgency and my impatience, and in response, he resisted. And finally, I snapped. I yelled, "Please just go to sleep!" The moment the words left my mouth, I knew I'd gone too far. His little lip quivered. His green eyes filled with tears. And then the worst thing happened—he asked me to leave his room and he went to sleep.

I spent the next hour and a half that I had been longing for completely racked with guilt. I knew he needed his one-on-one time with me. I knew how hard it was for him to stay home all day and share me with his little brother, who also happened to need extra holding. I was this three-year-old's whole world—his sun and moon—and I had yelled at him. And worse, he felt sad, and for the first time ever, he wanted to be alone rather than to be comforted by me. I had put a dent in our connection, and I knew it.

In that moment, I was faced with a painful realization that I wasn't the best mom and I probably was never going to be. I had once believed I could be—I'd always had a way with kids, received glowing reviews as a summer camp counselor and had spent hours playing with my niece and nephew, fully present and engaged.

But being a mom is different. I was making mistakes. I wasn't as patient as I thought I was. I wish I could say that this was the only time I've lost my cool, but it's not. In my worst moments, I've yelled, I've cursed and I've cried tears of pure frustration and overwhelm. I am far from perfect, and certainly not "the best," if such a thing even exists.

But I do try my best. I apologize when I'm wrong or when I lose my cool. I'm present when I'm with my kids, and I'll never stop striving to be better. I will always do what I believe is best for them, even when they don't like me for it. Even when "everyone else gets to stay up past their bedtime." I will always make the choices I think are best for them, whether they understand it in the moment or not.

I'm not perfect. But maybe they will never have to feel like they have to be perfect either. Maybe they're learning, just like I am, that it's okay to make mistakes and what really matters is how we repair them. Maybe we're teaching each other about grace and forgiveness. The more grace you give yourself, the more love and forgiveness you can freely offer them.

You don't have to be a perfect mom. There is no such thing. You'll make mistakes. And if you're anything like me, you'll make them again and again. But you also have to forgive yourself again and again. Before the forgiveness comes the reflection and that will help you get better at this. And you will get better at this and you might just learn to love yourself a little more in the process.

See page 190 for journal prompt.

AFTERWORD

So now that we've established that *being in the weeds will pass, we've found our people, showed our cards, brought our sexy back, nourished ourselves* and *forgiven ourselves again and again*—we have so much more to give to the little souls we're blessed with raising.

Now that we're a little more balanced, the more balanced we can become, and the more present we can be on this beautiful journey.

This is why I wrote this book.

Because I've been in the weeds, with no light in sight.

I've fought my way back—one careful, intentional move at a time.

I've traced the paths that led to my breaking point and learned how to avoid them, with the right care for myself.

And I've realized: the more I take care of me, the better I take care of my children.

When I fill myself with love and kindness, it can't help but spill over onto everyone in my home.

It is not selfish to care for your own soul—it is *essential*.

When you shine as brightly as you can, you illuminate the path for those walking beside you and for those coming after you.

You're also modeling the kind of self-care you want your children to one day give themselves so that the cycle can go on and on. That cycle begins with you.

Never stop filling your cup, so you always have something to pour from.

Learning how to put yourself first is not only the ultimate gift to your children—it's the ultimate lesson of motherhood.

I don't think it's accidental that we sometimes feel like we're losing a part of ourselves when we become mothers.

Because maybe we're not just birthing a new soul. Maybe we're birthing a new, more radiant version of ourselves, too.

Sometimes you have to lose something to find something even better.

Motherhood is the most amazing gift for so many reasons.

We hear about the beauty of bringing precious life into the world and the depth of unconditional love we can feel for another little human. Perhaps this is also a chance for you to learn to love yourself unconditionally as well.

This journey isn't just about becoming a mom.

It's about becoming a more fully dimensional version of yourself stretching not just your uterus, but your soul; filling not just your breasts, but your heart; strengthening not just your pelvic floor, but your resilience.

With the right words, awareness and tools, you now have the chance to raise not only a beautiful soul—but to protect and honor your own. The most rewarding things in life often feel like the hardest. Maybe that's because the reward isn't just in the outcome—but in the growing.

The seed of a flower begins in the weeds. But with the proper care, nourishment and time, it rises up in full bloom. It finds its moment in the sun and shares its beauty with the world.

And now, mama, so can you.

Come join me in the sun. I can see the light.

JOURNAL
PROMPTS

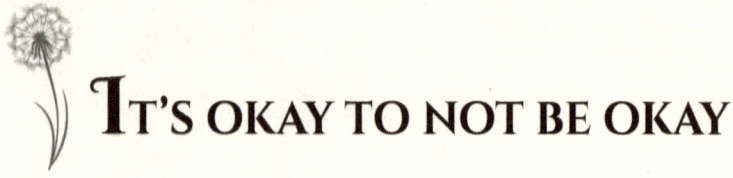

IT'S OKAY TO NOT BE OKAY

Take a few minutes to think about all the ways in which you feel like you are not okay right now. Write them all down; think of it as a way to release those thoughts from your mind and body onto the page and face them.

Now, read your list as if a friend were sharing it with you.
How does that change the way you feel about your list?

_____

_____

_____

_____

_____

_____

_____

_____

What words of support and compassion would you offer her?

_____

_____

_____

_____

_____

_____

Now, read those same words back to yourself—because you are
worthy of the same kindness and compassion.

TAKE A BREAK
BEFORE YOU BREAK

Take a look at your daily routine—where can you *realistically* carve out 20 minutes of quiet? Maybe it's early in the morning before the house wakes up, during nap time or after the kids go to bed. Maybe it's a midday reset while the baby naps—or even a few stolen moments in the car before walking back inside.

_____

_____

_____

_____

_____

_____

_____

_____

_____

_____

_____

_____

_____

Now that you have a time and a place, write it down here as a promise to yourself. Share it with your partner, kids or whoever makes up your support system. Make it *nonnegotiable.*

_____

_____

_____

_____

_____

_____

_____

_____

_____

_____

_____

_____

_____

_____

This is your time to reset—because you deserve it.

# FIND YOUR PEOPLE

Make a list of your closest people. Who do you turn to when you're not at your best?

_____

_____

_____

_____

_____

_____

_____

_____

_____

_____

_____

_____

_____

Do you usually feel seen and heard by this person or people? Identify who truly listens and validates you without judging.

_____

_____

_____

_____

_____

_____

_____

_____

_____

_____

_____

_____

_____

_____

If you don't have these answers now, just pay attention to how you feel after venting to each person, and identify your people based on that. Favorite their contacts so you can reach out to them right away when you need to.

FIND YOUR ZEN WHEREVER YOU CAN

Think back to the little things you used to love before life got busier—before kids, before your priorities shifted. What brought you joy, peace or a sense of contentment? Make a list of everything that comes to mind.

What is one thing you can adapt to add to your life now? Choose one small thing to add into your routine and pay close attention to how you feel afterwards.

_____

_____

_____

_____

_____

_____

_____

_____

_____

_____

_____

_____

_____

_____

_____

_____

_____

Remember, you should be at the top of your checklist.

WHEN IN DOUBT, DANCE!

Think about the music that instantly lifts your mood. Is there a song that makes you want to dance, a tune that helps you unwind or a playlist that just feels like home? Make a list of your go-to songs for different moods.

_____

_____

_____

_____

_____

_____

How can you bring more of that music into your daily routine?

_____

_____

_____

_____

_____

_____

Listen to one of your songs now, maybe even get up and dance around. How did that song shift your mood? Write about how you felt before-and how you feel now.

_____

_____

_____

_____

_____

_____

_____

_____

_____

_____

_____

_____

_____

_____

_____

_____

_____

_____

Now, never miss a chance to dance!

THIS TOO SHALL PASS

Write about one thing in your life that you once believed would never change—but did. Maybe you thought you'd never leave a certain job, never heal from a heartbreak or never feel good in your own body. And yet, time moved forward, and so did you.

_____

_____

_____

_____

_____

_____

_____

_____

_____

_____

_____

_____

_____

_____

What feels really hard right now?

_____

_____

_____

_____

_____

_____

_____

_____

_____

_____

_____

_____

_____

_____

_____

_____

_____

_____

Let it out and remember, this too shall pass.

Rest is best

Have you ever experienced a time when you felt so much better after a good night's sleep?

_____

_____

_____

_____

_____

_____

_____

_____

_____

_____

_____

_____

_____

_____

_____

_____

Who would you trust to look after your baby while you catch up on sleep? Now imagine you're asking them for help.

What feelings does asking for help bring up for you?

_____

_____

_____

_____

_____

_____

_____

_____

_____

_____

_____

_____

_____

_____

_____

Now take a deep breath and remind yourself that being vulnerable is an act of bravery, and taking care of yourself is essential to taking care of others. Remember, you can't pour from an empty cup.

STOP GIVING A F*CK WHAT OTHER PEOPLE THINK

Can you think of a time when you felt embarrassed or judged? Write about it in detail.

Now visualize that same situation—only instead, you just went about your business, laughed it off or offered a smile to whomever was doing the judging.

_____

_____

_____

_____

_____

_____

_____

_____

_____

_____

_____

_____

_____

_____

_____

Tap into that energy and watch your life change!

CHOOSE ONE THING

How do you feel physically?

_____

_____

_____

_____

_____

_____

_____

What is one thing you want to improve or change?

_____

_____

_____

_____

_____

_____

_____

Choose one daily challenge for yourself that will help you reach that goal in a short amount of time. Now think about how good you'll feel when you've accomplished that.

_____

_____

_____

_____

_____

_____

_____

_____

_____

_____

_____

_____

_____

_____

_____

Commit to your challenge and pat yourself on the back for completing it each day. Step into your power and enjoy!

DRESS FOR THE PART

When was the last time you left the house feeling like a million bucks? How did your overall appearance come together that day? Describe what you were wearing.

_____

_____

_____

_____

_____

_____

Now, take a good look at your closet and pull out the pieces you can realistically wear while momming. Do they make you feel good? If so, add them to your capsule closet.

_____

_____

_____

_____

_____

_____

Now, consider what's missing. Are there clothing items, shoes or accessories that would make getting dressed more fun? What about hair products, makeup or self-care essentials that help you feel more put together? Make a list of what you can invest in now and what you'd love to add to your wish list.

_____

_____

_____

_____

_____

_____

_____

_____

_____

_____

_____

_____

_____

_____

Because when you look good, you feel good—and you deserve to feel your best every day.

YOU CAN'T MAKE THIS SH*T UP

Can you think of one crazy "can't make this sh*t up" story from your past? Write about it.

_____

_____

_____

_____

_____

_____

_____

_____

_____

_____

_____

_____

_____

_____

How did you feel on the other side of it? Reminding yourself of how resilient you are can help you when these situations come up in motherhood.

_____

_____

_____

_____

_____

_____

_____

_____

_____

_____

_____

_____

_____

_____

Remember, we can do hard things. Bonus points if you can find the humor in it!

STAY ON YOUR OWN MAT

Reflect and write about a time you remember when you felt less than compared to someone else.

_____

_____

_____

_____

_____

_____

_____

_____

_____

_____

_____

_____

_____

_____

_____

Now, visualize that situation only this time, pick up your mat and move it to a place without comparison, a place where you can just focus on yourself.

Where else in your life can you prioritize your connection to yourself and stay on your own mat?

_____

_____

_____

_____

_____

_____

_____

_____

_____

_____

_____

_____

_____

_____

Remember, this is your time to unapologetically do what is best for you, because you matter too!

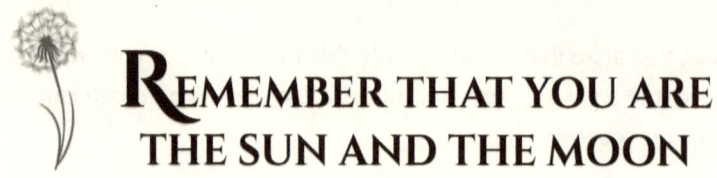

REMEMBER THAT YOU ARE THE SUN AND THE MOON

Think back to a time in your childhood when your parent or caregiver was sick, out of commission or just plain unavailable. Reflect on what emotions come up as you remember that experience and take a moment to write about them.

_____

_____

_____

_____

_____

_____

_____

_____

_____

_____

_____

_____

_____

_____

_____

_____

Now, reflect on how you are the sun and the moon in your child's life. How do you show up for them each day, even in the smallest ways?

_____

_____

_____

_____

_____

_____

_____

How can you celebrate the ways that you show up for your child and keep shining?

_____

_____

_____

_____

_____

_____

Keep shining bright!

THE HEAL IS REAL

Write about one thing from your own childhood you'd like to change—maybe it's a family tradition that you didn't love or the way someone in your family communicated. How can you make that change for your own child?

_____

_____

_____

_____

_____

_____

_____

_____

_____

_____

_____

_____

_____

Now write about something you loved from your own childhood. Make a promise to yourself to recreate that for your own child.

_____

_____

_____

_____

_____

_____

_____

_____

_____

_____

_____

_____

_____

_____

This may bring up emotions you weren't even aware were there. This is a good thing. Healing begins with feeling, so let it out. Your inner child will thank you.

IT'S A JUNGLE OUT THERE ON THE PLAYGROUND

Think about the friendships in your life that have meant the most to you. Write how you feel when you spend time with these friends and why. Are they funny, compassionate, real?

_____

_____

_____

_____

_____

_____

_____

_____

_____

_____

_____

_____

_____

_____

_____

_____

Have you found these same qualities in your mom friends? Do you bring these qualities to your friendships with other moms? If not, what is one way you can make an effort to be the mom friend that you'd like to have?

_____

_____

_____

_____

_____

_____

_____

_____

_____

_____

_____

_____

_____

_____

_____

_____

Remember, like attracts like. It starts with you.

FIND SOMETHING NEW

Make a list of all the things that interest you or that you have always wanted to try. The sky is the limit!

_____

_____

_____

_____

_____

_____

_____

_____

_____

_____

_____

_____

_____

_____

_____

Now, examine that list, see if you can find one thing that is doable right now, and make a commitment to yourself to do it. Maybe you can't hop on a plane to Italy, but maybe there's a local Italian cooking class you can try, or you could sign up for Duolingo and start learning to speak Italian.

_____

_____

_____

_____

_____

_____

_____

_____

_____

_____

_____

_____

_____

_____

Fitting in something new can help you discover a whole new side of yourself and balance out the mom brain. Don't be afraid to shake it up!

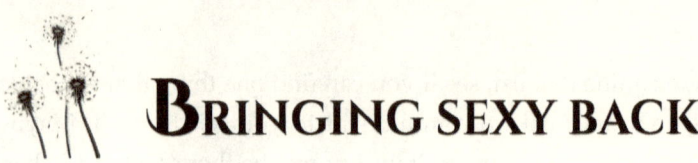

BRINGING SEXY BACK

Write about what sexy means to you. When was the last time you felt sexy?

If you feel brave, take a moment to look in the mirror after you step out of the shower and really see yourself.

_____

_____

_____

_____

_____

_____

_____

_____

_____

_____

_____

_____

_____

_____

Now, find three things to compliment and thank your body out loud for the amazing job it's doing.

_____

_____

_____

_____

_____

_____

_____

_____

_____

_____

_____

_____

_____

_____

_____

_____

_____

Embrace your new sexy and, if you feel called to do so, book that boudoir session or take your own!

TIME IS ON YOUR SIDE

What is one situation that feels overwhelming right now?

_____

_____

_____

_____

How can you break it down into smaller, more manageable pieces?

_____

_____

_____

_____

What's the next small step you can take today?

_____

_____

_____

_____

_____

Write down your plan to break down your week, your day or even the next hour if need be!

_____

_____

_____

_____

_____

_____

_____

_____

_____

_____

_____

_____

_____

_____

_____

_____

And remember, don't forget how far you've already come.

GRATITUDE WORKS!

Pause for a moment and list three things you're grateful for today. They can be big or small—anything that brings you comfort, joy or a moment of peace.

_____

_____

_____

_____

_____

_____

_____

_____

_____

_____

_____

_____

Now, read your list out loud and take a breath after each one. Let yourself truly feel the magnitude of your gratitude.

Next, think of something in your day that feels like an obligation. Write it down two ways: first, as a "have to," and then reframe it as a "get to."

_____

_____

_____

_____

_____

_____

Place your hand on your heart and read both versions out loud. Did you feel a shift in your body or your mood when you read the second sentence?

_____

_____

_____

_____

_____

_____

The more you practice this attitude of gratitude in your life, the simpler it becomes. Remember, you "get to" take care of yourself today.

THE MISSING PIECE

Pause for a moment and check in with yourself. What feeling do you miss most in this season of life? A sense of accomplishment? Creativity? Quiet? Connection?

_____

_____

_____

_____

_____

_____

_____

_____

_____

_____

_____

_____

_____

_____

Write about what's missing and brainstorm one small way to bring it back into your daily routine.

_____

_____

_____

_____

_____

_____

_____

_____

_____

_____

_____

_____

_____

_____

_____

_____

_____

_____

Remember, it's all about balance.

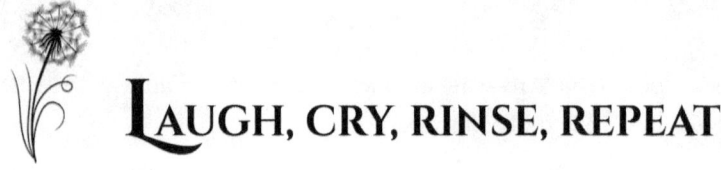

LAUGH, CRY, RINSE, REPEAT

When was the last time you had a good cry? Write about how you felt after.

_____

_____

_____

_____

_____

_____

_____

_____

_____

_____

_____

_____

_____

_____

_____

_____

_____

How can you create a quiet, safe space yourself to fully feel your emotions, even the uncomfortable ones? Let it flow and let it go!

_____

_____

_____

_____

_____

_____

_____

_____

_____

_____

_____

_____

_____

_____

_____

_____

_____

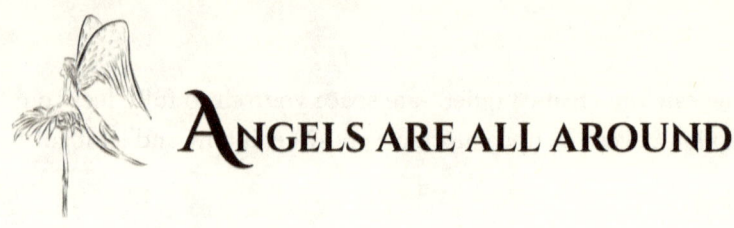

ANGELS ARE ALL AROUND

Write about one instance that comes to mind when you were the recipient of an unexpected act of kindness.

_____

_____

_____

_____

_____

_____

_____

_____

_____

_____

_____

_____

_____

_____

_____

Now write about when you were an angel to someone else.

_____

_____

_____

_____

_____

_____

_____

_____

_____

_____

_____

_____

_____

_____

_____

_____

_____

Commit to spending one day or an outing noticing acts of kindness around you. The more you notice them, the more they will appear.

Pick your poison

Make a list of tasks that need to be completed each day in order for you to feel at peace. Go about your day and take a mental note of when you find yourself doing something that brings you joy while thinking you "should be" completing one of your tasks.

_____

_____

_____

_____

_____

_____

_____

_____

_____

_____

_____

_____

_____

_____

Now make a plan for when the "should" can happen so you can be present and fully enjoy what you're doing in the moment.

_____

_____

_____

_____

_____

_____

_____

_____

_____

_____

_____

_____

_____

_____

_____

Pick your poison with intention.

NOURISH YOURSELF

Write about one nourishing meal that always hits the spot. Can you easily add it into your weekly rotation? If not, take some time to find a simple recipe that captures the essence of this meal. Social media and other online resources contain so many nourishing simple recipes that you can adapt to fit your schedule.

_____

_____

_____

_____

_____

_____

_____

_____

_____

_____

_____

_____

_____

_____

Now, take a few minutes to examine your vices. Be honest with yourself and really listen to your inner voice. Are there any habits or coping mechanisms that are doing more harm than good?

_____

_____

_____

_____

_____

_____

_____

_____

_____

_____

_____

_____

_____

_____

_____

_____

Remember, nourishing your child begins with nourishing yourself.

SHOW YOUR CARDS

When was the last time you let yourself be truly honest with someone? Think back to a moment when you weren't doing so well —when you dropped the mask and shared how you were really feeling instead of defaulting to "fine" or "great." What happened next? How did it feel to be that honest? Now, take a moment to write about how it might feel to be that open with someone again today.

_____

_____

_____

_____

_____

_____

_____

_____

_____

_____

_____

_____

_____

What are you really feeling today? Instead of defaulting to "fine" or "good," take a moment to truly check in with yourself—and be honest. Are you tired? Peaceful? Frustrated? Content? Let whatever is true for you rise to the surface, without editing or judgment, and write it down. Then, try practicing saying it out loud, just as you would if someone asked how you're doing. Let yourself speak from that place of truth.

_____

_____

_____

_____

_____

_____

_____

_____

_____

_____

_____

_____

_____

_____

_____

Remember, you are not alone.

EMBRACE THE SOUL
YOU ARE RAISING

Think back to when you were growing up. Write about what interested you.

_____

_____

_____

_____

_____

_____

_____

_____

_____

_____

_____

_____

_____

_____

_____

_____

What were you drawn to? Did you feel like those sparks were always celebrated? How were they celebrated? Make a promise to yourself to catch as many glimpses of your own child as possible and commit to always honoring them.

_____

_____

_____

_____

_____

_____

_____

_____

_____

_____

_____

_____

_____

_____

_____

Sit back, relax and enjoy the show!

SURRENDER

Write about one stressful situation in your life. List the "what ifs" from a place of stress. Now take a deep breath and make another list leaning into the positive "what ifs." Read each list and be mindful of how it makes you feel.

_____

_____

_____

_____

_____

_____

_____

_____

_____

_____

_____

_____

_____

Now make another list. What was actually in your control in that situation? What wasn't? Letting go of what you cannot control is the power of surrender.

_____

_____

_____

_____

_____

_____

_____

_____

_____

_____

_____

_____

_____

_____

_____

_____

_____

Continue to practice the sweet surrender.

BOUNDARIES,
BOUNDARIES, BOUNDARIES!

Reflect on what it means to you to set a boundary. What feelings does that bring up for you? Do you feel anxious or intimidated?

_____

_____

_____

_____

_____

_____

_____

_____

_____

_____

_____

_____

_____

_____

_____

_____

Think of an area in your life where you feel resentful and that might be the place where you need to set a healthy boundary. Write down your boundary and practice saying it aloud without guilt or the need to explain your reasoning. How did that feel? Keep practicing—boundaries, boundaries, boundaries!

_____

_____

_____

_____

_____

_____

_____

_____

_____

_____

_____

_____

_____

_____

_____

Remember, you are not building a wall, you are building a bridge.

DON'T POOH-POOH
THE WOO

What's one unconventional or "woo woo" practice you've been curious about but haven't tried yet? What's holding you back—fear of judgment, skepticism, time or something else?

_____

_____

_____

_____

_____

_____

_____

_____

_____

_____

_____

_____

_____

_____

_____

How might it feel to give yourself permission to explore it anyway, just for you?

_____

_____

_____

_____

_____

_____

_____

_____

_____

_____

_____

_____

_____

_____

_____

_____

Keep an open mind and embrace the woo!

FORGIVE YOURSELF AGAIN AND AGAIN

Write about a time you made a mistake.

Have you forgiven yourself?

Visualize a close friend or even your own grown child making the same mistake. What would you say to them? Was it something kinder than what you said to yourself? Extend yourself the same grace and kindness, and practice the beautiful art of forgiving yourself.

_____

_____

_____

_____

_____

_____

_____

_____

_____

_____

_____

_____

_____

_____

Now forgive yourself again and again.

ACKNOWLEDGMENTS

Thank you, thank you, thank you to some pretty amazing people.

My greatest gifts in the world: my two sons, Winston and Hudson: without you two I would have no stories from motherhood to tell. Being your mom is my greatest blessing. Thank you for your love, your hugs and your patience as I strive to be the mother you deserve.

My husband, Joe: thank you for believing in me, encouraging me to go for it and giving me the space and time to create.

My mom, Kathleen: thank you for giving me a solid foundation and teaching me how to lead with kindness and mother with unconditional love.

Daddy: thank you for always encouraging my love of books and inspiring me to create and embrace my authenticity unapologetically.

My friends and fellow moms: especially Brook who made me feel so seen and validated that "dark hole" day: thank you for supporting my writing, validating my experiences and helping me laugh through the crazy.

The team at Legacy Launch Pad Publishing: especially Anna David and Jennifer Horan, thank you for believing in my book and making my dream a reality.

To my favorite authors and beautiful truth-tellers who paved the way and showed me how TMI can actually be incredibly healing: especially Glennon Doyle, Elizabeth Gilbert, Brené Brown and Chelsea Handler, thank you for lighting the way for me to share my truth and own my stories.

And to all the moms who found this: together we can change the world by raising beautiful souls while rescuing our own. You are not alone.

ABOUT THE AUTHOR

 Cindy Caprio Woulfe is a full-time mother, a certified meditation teacher and wellness advocate residing in Connecticut with her husband and two sons. A University of Colorado at Boulder graduate in Communication and Institute of Integrative Nutrition alumna, she balances motherhood with her passion for mindfulness practices.

Through her writing, she offers compassionate guidance for mothers seeking balance amid life's overwhelming moments. She is a regular contributor to *Fairfield County Mom*. *In the Weeds* is her first book.

ABOUT THE PUBLISHER

Legacy Launch Pad is a boutique publishing company that works with entrepreneurs from all over the world. For more information about Legacy Launch Pad Publishing, go to: www.legacylaunchpadpub.com.